LOS ANGELES CHARGERS

BY JOSH ANDERSON

Stride
An Imprint of The Child's World®
childsworld.com

The Child's World
childsworld.com

Published by The Child's World®
800-599-READ • www.childsworld.com

Photography Credits
Cover: © Sean M. Haffey / Staff / Getty Images; page 1: © Africa Studio / Shutterstock; page 3: © Ralph Freso / Stringer / Getty Images; page 5: © Mike Ehrmann / Staff / Getty Images; page 6: © George Rose / Stringer / Getty Images; page 9: © Sam Greenwood / Staff / Getty Images; page 10: © Stephen Dunn / Staff / Getty Images; page 11: © stevezmina1 / Getty Images; page 12: © Jack Thomas / Stringer / Getty Images; page 12: © Mitchell Leff / Stringer / Getty Images; page 13: © Peter Read Miller / Associated Press; page 13: © Jeff Gross / Stringer / Getty Images; page 14: © Joe Scarnici / Stringer / Getty Images; page 15: © Jeff Gross / Staff / Getty Images; page 16: © Mike Powell / Staff / Getty Images; page 16: © Nick Laham / Staff / Getty Images; page 17: © Rob Carr / Staff / Getty Images; page 17: © Donald Miralle / Staff / Getty Images; page 18: © SportsChrome / Newscom; page 18: © Streeter Lecka / Staff / Getty Images; page 19: © Rob Carr / Staff / Getty Images; page 19: © Staff / Getty Images; page 20: © Harry How / Staff / Getty Images; page 20: © Sean M. Haffey / Staff / Getty Images; page 21: © Rob Carr / Staff / Getty Images; page 21: © Harry How / Staff / Getty Images; page 22: © Jim McIsaac / Staff / Getty Images; page 23: © Todd Warshaw / Stringer / Getty Images; page 23: © stevezmina1 / Getty Images; page 25: © Simon Bruty / Staff / Getty Images; page 26: © Al Messerschmidt Archive / Associated Press; page 29: © Stephen Dunn / Staff / Getty Images

ISBN Information
9781503857810 (Reinforced Library Binding)
9781503860544 (Portable Document Format)
9781503861909 (Online Multi-user eBook)
9781503863262 (Electronic Publication)

LCCN 2021952670

Printed in the United States of America

BRINGING THE WORLD 19 68 TO YOUNG READERS

TABLE OF CONTENTS

GO CHARGERS!

The Los Angeles Chargers compete in the National Football **League's** (NFL's) American Football Conference (AFC). They play in the AFC West **division**, along with the Denver Broncos, Kansas City Chiefs, and Las Vegas Raiders. The team recently left the city of San Diego, California, which had been home to the Chargers for more than 50 years. Now the Chargers are one of two NFL teams in Los Angeles. They share the city with the Los Angeles Rams. Let's learn more about the Chargers!

AFC EAST DIVISION

Denver Broncos

Kansas City Chiefs

Las Vegas Raiders

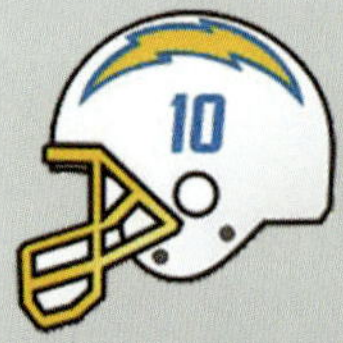

Los Angeles Chargers

THE CHARGERS STARTED IN LOS ANGELES IN 1960 AND RETURNED THERE IN 2017 AFTER 56 SEASONS IN SAN DIEGO.

BECOMING THE CHARGERS

The Chargers began play in 1960 as an original member of the American Football League (AFL). Before moving to San Diego in 1961, they played one season in Los Angeles. The Chargers played in the AFL Championship Game in five of the league's ten seasons, winning the big game once. The Chargers became a part of the NFL when the two leagues combined in 1970. The team moved back to Los Angeles before the 2017 season.

THE CHARGERS LEAD THE NFL IN PASSING YARDS FROM 1978 TO 1983.

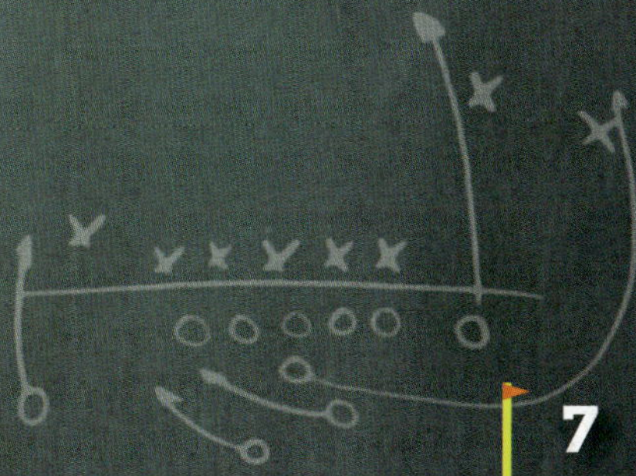

BY THE NUMBERS

The Chargers have played in **ONE** Super Bowl.

TEN
AFC West division titles for the Chargers

492
points scored by the team in 2006—a Chargers record!

TEN
Chargers enshrined in the Pro Football **Hall of Fame**

RUNNING BACK AUSTIN EKELER TOTALED 1,558 YARDS IN 2021.

PLAYER INTRODUCTIONS AT SOFI STADIUM GET FANS EXCITED FOR THE UPCOMING GAME.

GAME DAY

The Chargers play in Inglewood, California, which is in Los Angeles County. The team has played its home games at SoFi **Stadium** since 2020 when the building was completed. SoFi is also home to the NFL's Los Angeles Rams. On game days, SoFi Stadium holds a little more than 70,000 fans. The stadium is covered by a clear plastic roof that lets in plenty of light. The Chargers' first game at SoFi was an **overtime** loss to the Kansas City Chiefs.

We're Famous!

A Chargers jersey makes an appearance in the beloved 1984 film, *The Karate Kid*. Daniel LaRusso, played by Ralph Macchio, wears a number 89 Chargers jersey as he tries to outrun a group of bullies. At the time the film was made, that jersey number belonged to four-time **Pro Bowl** wide receiver Wes Chandler.

UNIFORM

Truly Weird

A Chargers kickoff in 1983 was once completely lost to history. Down 27–22 against the New York Jets, the Chargers' kicker pinned the Jets deep on their own side of the field. But the TV station playing the game was on a commercial break. League officials asked for a re-kick. This time, the Jets returned the ball far into Chargers territory. The Jets scored and went on to win the game 41–29.

Alternate Jersey

Sometimes teams wear an alternate jersey that is different from their home and away jerseys. It might be a bright color or have a unique theme. During the 2020 season, the Chargers wore their dark blue uniforms for a game against the Atlanta Falcons. The new look proved lucky. The Chargers won 20–17.

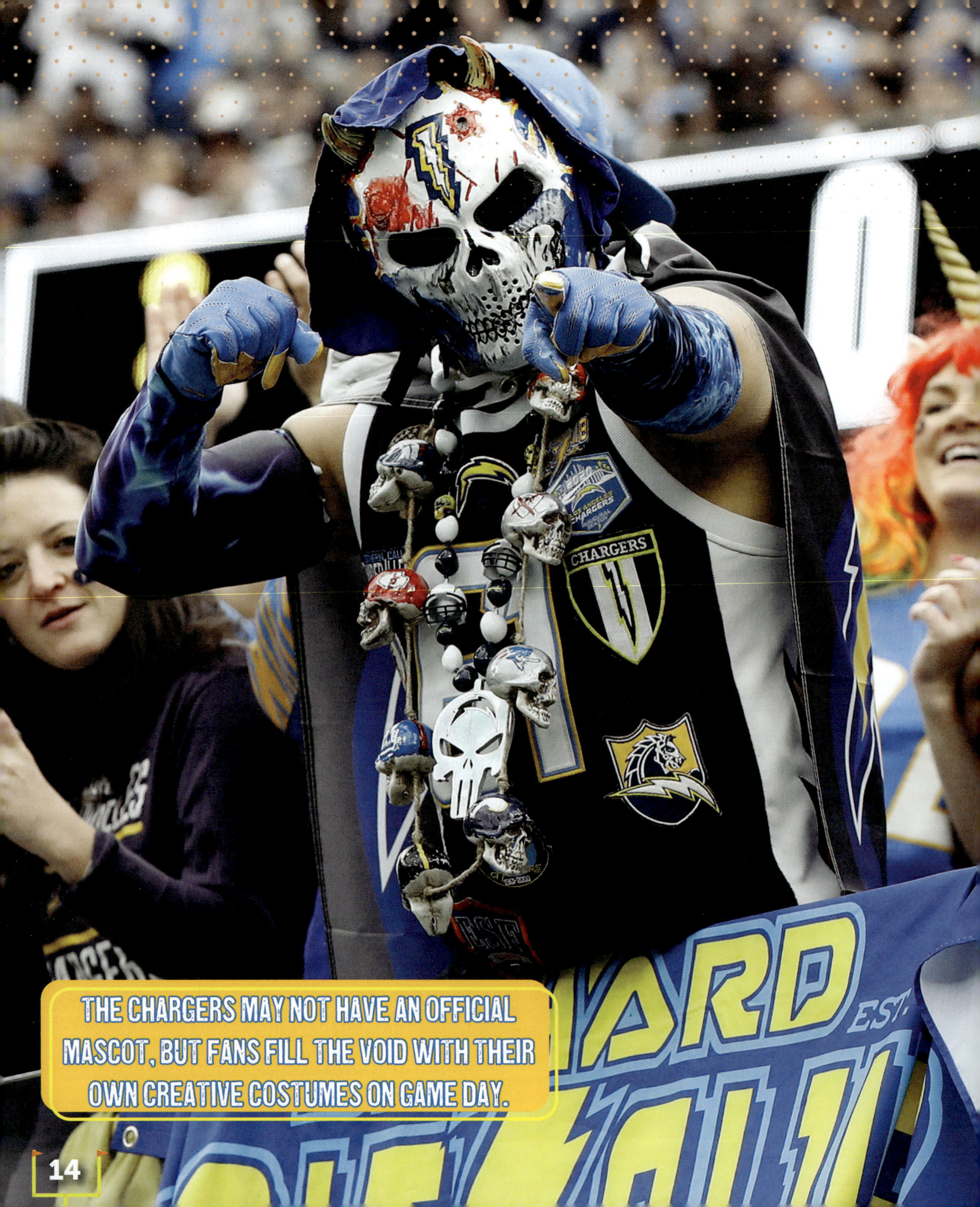

THE CHARGERS MAY NOT HAVE AN OFFICIAL MASCOT, BUT FANS FILL THE VOID WITH THEIR OWN CREATIVE COSTUMES ON GAME DAY.

TEAM SPIRIT

Going to a game at SoFi Stadium can be loads of fun. Before the game, fans can tailgate in one of SoFi's designated spaces and enjoy food and drinks brought from home. Inside the stadium, the Charger Girls cheerleading squad entertains fans during breaks in the action. While the team doesn't have an official mascot, a lifelong fan of the team helped to fill the void for many years. Boltman would appear at Chargers games in a bright homemade costume. Hungry fans should not miss the cheeseburger sub or deep-fried hot dog at SoFi's LA Eats location.

BOLTMAN

HEROES OF HISTORY

Dan Fouts
Quarterback | 1973–1987

Fouts was chosen for the Pro Bowl six times and led the Chargers to three AFC West titles. He led the NFL in passing yards in four straight seasons from 1979 to 1982. Fouts was inducted into the Pro Football Hall of Fame in 1993.

Antonio Gates
Tight End | 2003–2018

Gates ranks first among tight ends and seventh overall in league history with 116 **touchdown** catches. The eight-time Pro Bowler is the Chargers' all-time leader in catches (955), receiving yards (11,841), and receiving touchdowns (116). Gates helped lead the Chargers to the **playoffs** seven times.

Philip Rivers

Quarterback | 2004–2019

Rivers ranks sixth all-time in passing yards (63,440) and passing touchdowns (421). As their starting quarterback, he led the Chargers to four AFC West division titles and six playoff appearances. The team won 123 games with Rivers at quarterback. He was chosen for the Pro Bowl eight times.

Junior Seau

Linebacker | 1990–2002

A 12-time Pro Bowler, Seau led the defense that took the Chargers to their first-ever **Super Bowl** in 1994. He was chosen as one of the NFL's 100 greatest players of all time. Seau was inducted into the Pro Football Hall of Fame in 2015.

The Chargers defeat the Boston Patriots 51–10 to win the AFL Championship.

Philip Rivers throws three touchdown passes in a victory over the Indianapolis Colts. The win earns the Chargers a spot in the AFC Championship Game.

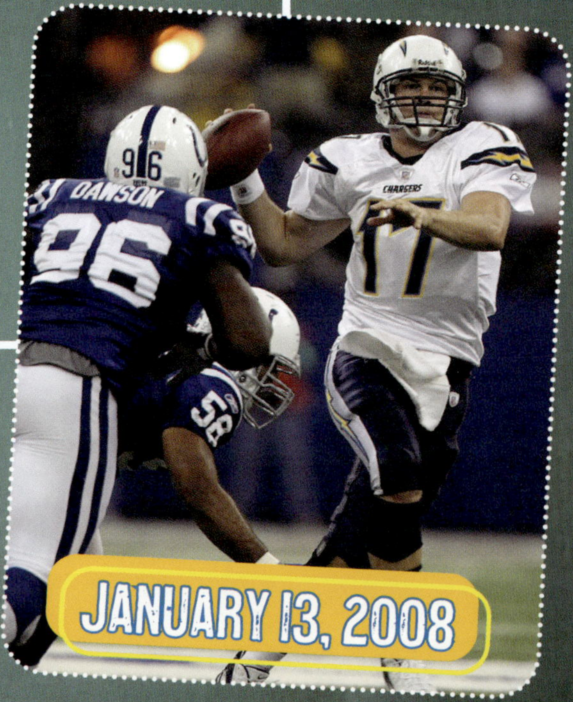

BIG DAYS

JANUARY 6, 2019

The Chargers defeat the Baltimore Ravens 23–17 in a Wild Card playoff game. It's the final playoff victory for Chargers legend Antonio Gates.

APRIL 23, 2020

With the sixth pick in the first round of the NFL Draft, the Chargers select quarterback Justin Herbert. Herbert starts 15 games as a **rookie**.

MODERN-DAY MARVELS

Keenan Allen

Wide Receiver | Debut: 2013

Allen was selected to five straight Pro Bowls from 2017 to 2021. His 624 catches through the first 100 games of his career are the most of any player in league history. Allen had 16 catches in a 2020 game against the Jets—the most ever by a Charger.

Joey Bosa

Defensive End | Debut: 2016

Bosa compiled 58 **sacks** through his first six seasons with the Chargers. His impact on the defensive line earned him four trips to the Pro Bowl in his first six years. He forced seven fumbles during the 2021 season.

Justin Herbert

Quarterback | Debut: 2020

Herbert took over as the Chargers' starting quarterback in the second game of his rookie season. Herbert set the NFL rookie record with 31 passing touchdowns and eight 300-yard passing games in 2020. He was 2020's Offensive Rookie of the Year. He improved in 2021, throwing 38 touchdown passes and earning his first trip to the Pro Bowl.

Derwin James Jr.

Safety | Debut: 2018

In 2018, James became the first Chargers rookie to be named a starter in the Pro Bowl since 2005. He posted more than 100 tackles as a rookie and also had three interceptions. James was the first defensive back in history with three sacks in his first four games.

LADAINIAN TOMLINSON AVERAGED MORE THAN ONE TOUCHDOWN PER GAME DURING HIS NINE SEASONS WITH THE CHARGERS.

THE GOAT

GREATEST OF ALL TIME

LADAINIAN TOMLINSON

Only one player in league history has more rushing touchdowns than the 145 Tomlinson scored in his career. Tomlinson also ranks third all-time, with 162 total touchdowns. In 2006, "L. T." set records for the most rushing touchdowns (28) and total touchdowns (31) in a single season. His 13,684 rushing yards rank seventh all-time. Tomlinson is a five-time Pro Bowler and was elected to the Pro Football Hall of Fame in 2017.

FAN FAVORITE

Danny Woodhead–Running Back

2013–2016

Although Woodhead missed nearly two full seasons due to injury during his time as a Charger, he was beloved by fans for his toughness. Standing only 5 feet, 8 inches (173 cm) tall, Woodhead was one of the smaller running backs in the league. In 2013, he was second in the NFL for receiving touchdowns by a running back, with six.

THE BIG GAME

JANUARY 15, 1995 – AFC CHAMPIONSHIP GAME

Coming into their AFC Championship matchup with the Pittsburgh Steelers, the Chargers had never played in a Super Bowl before. The Chargers didn't lead until late in the fourth quarter. With about five minutes left, quarterback Stan Humphries found wide receiver Tony Martin for a 43-yard touchdown. The Chargers took the lead 17–13. But the Steelers marched all the way down the field and had a chance to win the game with about a minute left. Chargers linebacker Dennis Gibson knocked a pass away in the end zone on fourth down to seal the victory. The Chargers were headed for the Super Bowl!

THE STEELERS AND CHARGERS HAVE PLAYED THREE TIMES IN THE PLAYOFFS. THE CHARGERS HAVE WON TWO OF THE GAMES.

HEAD COACH SID GILLMAN LED THE CHARGERS TO 86 WINS BETWEEN 1960 AND 1971.

AMAZING FEATS

27
Touchdown Passes

In 1968 by
QUARTERBACK
John Hadl

1,350
Rushing Yards

In 1994 by
RUNNING BACK
Natrone Means

1,602
Receiving Yards

In 1965 by
WIDE RECEIVER
Lance Alworth

17
Sacks

In 1992 by
DEFENSIVE END
Leslie O'Neal

ALL-TIME BEST

PASSING YARDS

Philip Rivers
59,271

Dan Fouts
43,040

John Hadl
26,938

RUSHING YARDS

LaDainian Tomlinson
12,490

Paul Lowe
4,972

Marion Butts
4,297

RECEIVING YARDS

Antonio Gates
11,841

Lance Alworth
9,584

Charlie Joiner
9,203

SACKS*

Leslie O'Neal
105.5

Shaun Phillips
69.5

Gary Johnson
67.5

SCORING

John Carney
1,076

LaDainian Tomlinson
918

Nate Kaeding
889

INTERCEPTIONS

Gill Byrd
42

Dick Harris
29

Rodney Harrison
26

*unofficial before 1982

DEFENSIVE END LESLIE O'NEAL PLAYED FOR THE CHARGERS FROM 1986 UNTIL 1995.

GLOSSARY

division (dih-VIZSH-un): a group of teams within the NFL who play each other more frequently and compete for the best record

Hall of Fame (HAHL of FAYM): a museum in Canton, Ohio, that honors the best players in NFL history

league (LEEG): an organization of sports teams that compete against each other

overtime (OH-vuhr-tym): extra time that is played when teams are tied at the end of four quarters

playoffs (PLAY-ahfs): a series of games after the regular season that decides which two teams play in the Super Bowl

Pro Bowl (PRO BOWL): the NFL's All-Star game where the best players in the league compete

rookie (RUH-kee): a player playing in his first season

sack (SAK): when a quarterback is tackled behind the line of scrimmage before he can throw the ball

stadium (STAY-dee-uhm): a building with a field and seats for fans where teams play

Super Bowl (SOO-puhr BOWL): the championship game of the NFL, played between the winners of the AFC and the NFC

touchdown (TUTCH-down): a play in which the ball is brought into the other team's end zone, resulting in six points

FIND OUT MORE

IN THE LIBRARY

Bulgar, Beth and Mark Bechtel. *My First Book of Football.* New York, NY: Time Inc. Books, 2015.

Jacobs, Greg. *The Everything Kids' Football Book, 7th Edition*. Avon, MA: Adams Media, 2021.

Sports Illustrated Kids. *The Greatest Football Teams of All Time*. New York, NY: Time Inc. Books, 2018.

Wyner, Zach. *Los Angeles Chargers*. New York, NY: AV2, 2020.

ON THE WEB

Visit our website for links about the Los Angeles Chargers:
childsworld.com/links

Note to parents, teachers, and librarians: We routinely verify our web links to make sure they are safe and active sites. Encourage your readers to check them out!

INDEX

ABOUT THE AUTHOR

Josh Anderson has published over 50 books for children and young adults. His two boys are the greatest joys in his life. Hobbies include coaching his sons in youth basketball, no-holds-barred games of Apples to Apples, and taking long family walks. His favorite NFL team is a secret he'll never share!